ZOMBIE DEER
AND THE
BROW TINE BUCK
A TRUE STORY

JOSEPH DANIEL BYLER

TABLE OF CONTENTS

INTRODUCTION

My name is Joseph Byler. I have been an archer since I was young, thanks to the love of hunting my dad instilled in me while growing up. We have an Amish background, and the majority of my family still remains Amish today. As you might imagine, our love of the outdoors is in our blood and traditions.

I have always enjoyed every part of being an outdoorsman. It brings a feeling of freedom and relief that many people don't have the opportunity to experience, and it's something I don't take for granted.

I believe that getting out in God's awesome country, with no other purpose but to spend time in His presence, in the great creation He made, is more than enough reason for me.

No matter what time, rhyme, or reason I am in the woods, I can always learn something new, and I believe that none of that time is wasted! I believe every single hunt, even the unsuccessful ones, is still worth the time spent because each experience is a benefit and provides learning opportunities.

I hope you enjoy this story of a buck that I learned many new things from. I'm excited to relive the journey and share it with you!

CHAPTER 1

How It All Began, Fall 2007

It all began on a warm, beautiful Michigan morning in the fall of 2007. On this particular morning, I decided to change things up a bit, and hunt on the ground. The property I was hunting on had a small and worn-out apple orchard on a hillside, with a very large swamp along the bottom of a ridge.

There were many trails weaving throughout that small parcel, so I knew the deer were traveling back and forth in this area. I sat under a tree with thick brush surrounding me. There was an opening directly in front of me, which meant I could solely focus on one particular deer trail.

As the sun began to rise, the deer started funneling in one by one. I was amazed by the number of deer that traveled down this trail, especially the 1½-year-old bucks. I had never seen this many young bucks within a few hours of hunting before.

As I watched these young bucks walk by, I began dreaming of what the next few years could look like. I imagined these young ones growing into mature, big-boned monsters, which was sure to make the upcoming hunting seasons full of surprises and excitement.

My dad and I started practicing Quality Deer Management (QDMA) in 1999, but we have experienced a few challenges:

1. We only had approximately 30 acres to work with.
2. We have around 20 neighboring hunters in the surrounding 70-80 acres who do not practice QDMA.
3. Following the QDMA protocol can take time to develop into something special.

These things are super frustrating! *Seriously* – it sucks when you spend the time and money to plant food plots and establish mineral sites; put in the effort to try and harvest a mature buck on limited acreage; and deal with an excessive number of hunters and their individual, incompetent hunting beliefs.

My train of thought was suddenly derailed when I heard something coming through the brush. The noise startled me, and my heart started to race as it grew closer. I was on pins and needles because the amount of brush surrounding me made it hard to see anything.

Suddenly, a wide-eyed 1½-year-old buck pushed his head through the brush and stood there, frozen. He looked like he was mounted on a log-cabin wall. Being only a few feet away from each other, we locked eyes immediately and stared at each other with tunnel vision.

After a moment, the buck backed out and began circling around me through the brush, making every noise a white-tailed deer can make, and some odd ones that make me want to scratch my head. I wonder what goes through a wild animal's head sometimes.

Watching this young buck do his mysterious dance was both interesting and awkward. Observing him in this seemingly startled state was something new for me, and I was quickly taking mental notes. His actions and body language were very different from the other deer I had encountered before, and he had a curious personality and funny demeanor. He had a noticeably longer brow tine on his right side; and a short, stout and wide body. His unique characteristics made it easy to identify him.

He stayed within ten yards from me and continued his shenanigans before finally deciding to walk off. He made quite an impression on me. While I had hoped to see his grandpa lurking about, I understood that my interaction with him was extremely valuable.

On my walk back home, I realized that while this buck was young and immature, he had just taught me more about deer behavior than any other buck I've ever encountered while hunting.

CHAPTER 2

The Brow Tine Buck, The Rut of 2007

I saw the young buck about six more times over the next couple weeks, sparring with other small bucks and running with some does around the old apple orchard. He acted like that area of land was his to lock down, claiming it like he was Mel Gibson in *Braveheart*.

I decided to hunt on the ground in the evening, on one of the last days of the rut that bow season. I had seen a very large mature buck in the same area, but had left that space alone for the most part until the full swing of the rut.

I grabbed my gear and set up an awesome spot down at the bottom of a ridge, where I can see everything in front of me. Most hunters I know don't like to hunt on the ground, but it's a strategy I personally like to use. I like it for a few reasons, one of which has to do with a tree-stand accident where my survival was nothing short of a miracle (but that's a story for another time).

I hung up my bow, backpack, rattle bag, grunt calls, and all the other tools we hunters use to lure in the animal we are hunting. I take so much gear with me that sometimes I feel like I'm hunting in the mountains out west!

I thought of trying something new to lure the deer in. I decided to create a barrier to make myself scent-free when I set up for the hunt that evening.

I used a popular deer attractant and sprayed a perimeter around my 20-yard shooting area. I sprayed everything – trees, branches, leaves, etc. I saturated that area like I was killing bugs in my backyard. Lastly, I sprayed the soles of my boots before walking directly back to my hunting gear.

That night, I felt like a genius. I thought to my-self, *What a great idea this will be! Not only will I be scent-free, but the deer will also love smelling this attractant! They will be aroused with curiosity!*

As the sun set and daylight began to fade, I gave a couple grunts and hoped for one last chance to lure in a buck before gathering up my gear and heading home.

Suddenly, I heard a deer coming through the thickets from the other side of the ridge. It got clos-er and closer. Leaves were crunching, and then I heard grunting.

Yes! I thought. *My plan is working! I am the smartest hunter ever! Just wait until I show everyone this buck and tell them about my newly discovered amazing strategy!*

Nervous excitement rose within me, and my pride began to soar. This foolproof plan of mine was working out right before my very eyes! I was sure my monster buck and my strategy would be-come a nationwide sensation.

He snorted, sprayed, grunted, twitched, stomped, and appeared.

My eyebrows went up and my mouth dropped open as I feasted my eyes on knobby knees and big ears. To my surprise, it was that young and awkward brow tine buck!

I could barely believe my eyes! He started acting like the big man on campus, tearing limbs from trees and ripping up the ground. I could tell that he truly believed he was a boss.

His nose went up in the air, catching wind of something sweet. He slammed his nose to the ground like a dog chasing a jackrabbit. The attractant aroused him, and he started his shenanigans all over again.

Acting like a child in gym class playing duck-duck-goose, he walked and trotted around the perimeter where I had sprayed. Round and round he went. Flicking his tongue and licking the air, he tasted the fragrance that permeated every square inch of his immediate surroundings. Like walking into a Jimmy John's franchise, this guy was here for the *free smells*, not another deer encounter.

The evening grew darker, and a bright, night-time mercury light turned on at the property next to me.

Finally the young brow tine buck slowed down and turned directly toward me. He took one step, then another, and stopped 10 feet of me, still nose-to-the-ground licking and smelling the area where I saturated my boots with attractant. Based on the way he was acting, I became concerned that he would attack me, and I started thinking things might not turn out so well.

Annoyed by his rigmarole, I decided I wasn't going to just stand there all night with my bow in hand and arrow pointed. All of a sudden, he looked up and stared right at me. He took a step toward me, and another, and another. Finally, he stopped less then a foot from my 2-Blade Stinger Buzzcut Broadhead. Again, we were at a standoff just like earlier in the year. My heart and mind were racing as we stood in the dark - man versus wild animal, in the middle of the woods, boots to hooves, pred- ator and prey, history in the making.

Acting fast, I lunged forward and yelled the first thing that came to mind - *WHOOOOM!!!*

At the sound of surprise bellowing, he fell back- ward and began rolling over and over as if he were doing a gymnastics floor exercise at the Olympics. Once he got back on his hooves, he started falling forward. Then he was rolling face first, flipping over the fencerow toward the mercury light.

All I could see were leaves and dirt scattering everywhere, and the young buck having what seemed like an out-of-body experience in the shadows.

At this, I quickly gathered my gear and started my hike back home.

All sorts of emotions were flowing through my body. I was totally unsure of what in the world was going on with this curious deer. That was the evening when I officially named him "The Brow Tine Buck".

That night, a few things came to mind while looking back at that night's events:

1. I don't think this crazy method will work with a smart, mature buck. At all. Like, ever!
2. I really hope I keep seeing this young buck.
3. That was still an awesome experience, and I am pumped to see him develop into a brute.

I was just excited to learn, and felt like I had a somewhat weird connection with such an animal.

A week later, during shotgun season, I saw The Brow Tine Buck one last time. It seemed his eyes were looking into the twilight zone. Every noise he heard seemed to send him in panic mode, and he acted scared out of his mind. But I figured his scaredy-cat mindset would go away as soon as he grew a nice rack and forgot the entire fiasco from this season.

The following deer season, I never saw The Brow Tine Buck. Not on the trail camera, or at the mineral site, or the food plot. I became discouraged and started thinking that he had been shot or hit by a car. But things changed for the better during the 2009 bow season.

CHAPTER 3

Fighting Emotions, The Rut of 2009

I was sitting in my favorite tree stand during the late bow-season rut. I prayed for an opportunity not only to kill a nice buck, but to also encounter The Brow Tine Buck again, if he were alive. If he did happen to be out there somewhere, he would be 3½ years old, and in Michigan, that means I better lay the hammer down.

Eagerly, I gave a couple grunts and a few rattles. In the distance, I heard deer racing through the swamp, the sound of a buck running after another.

Almost instantly, two mature bucks were fighting right in front of me. They were giving it their all, and watching them made my heart race!

One buck pushed the other one over with his rack. The one who was pushed over twisted around and, with his large rack, positioned himself under the other's hind end and chased it out of the clearing.

The winning buck suddenly put on the brakes. He stood there victoriously and watched the loser run for his life. But he was also very still, like he was waiting for his gold medal in fencing.

As I watched him, I felt that there was something familiar about him. I stared intently, and I couldn't shake the feeling that I knew him. Even though some time had passed, I knew this buck just like I knew the back of my own hand. There was no doubt in my mind. This was my Brow Tine Buck! Now mature and old enough to harvest, he was a perfect eight-point.

In my moment of realization, all the feelings and emotions I had for this animal came washing over me. I felt frozen. *This is my chance*, I thought.

While he was not out of shooting range with my bow, I was faced with a problem. I didn't have a clear shot because I had so many tree limbs in the way. I weighed my options and considered just taking the bad shot and hoping for the best.

I stood on my seat to see if a clear shot was possible, but it wasn't. Secured by my Muddy Outdoor tree harness, I leaned out the side of the tree stand, attempting to get a shot, but quickly decided that angle wouldn't work, either.

Anxiousness rose within me. There was absolutely no good shot! Mad at myself for not prepping the stand better, I hung up my bow, and began watching my buck scrape and thrash every single thing in his sight for the next 40 minutes, maybe longer.

He began taunting me. All I could do was sit there, learn from his actions, and watch my dreams of shooting him and dragging him home pass me by.

The following lesson was learned during that day's frustrating events: next time, do a better job of preparing the shooting lanes. It sickened me to watch him eventually walk back into the swamp of sorrows.

This Brow Tine Buck became an obsession to me. I started hearing many stories from the neighboring hunters. They talked about how they saw a big eight-point with a bit of a different brow tine on his rack running does around the field; and how vehicles were parked along the side of the road, watching this unique buck eat in the field at night.

That was *my* deer they were talking about! I knew it! And this should be *my* time in the woods with this deer! I was beyond frustrated at this point. This was *my* story to tell, not theirs!

I never encountered The Brow Tine Buck for the rest of the 2009 season. Sadly, the following two years went by with absolutely zero sign of him.

I was really hoping to see him during hunting season. He was a special buck, and I wanted to have him mounted on my wall. But I felt discouraged, believing that someone else had killed him.

CHAPTER 4

QDMA and Minerals,
January 2011

As I mentioned earlier, my dad and I stopped shooting small bucks back in 1999 and started practicing
QDMA. This was a new philosophy at the time, and
passing up bucks of any size back then was frowned
upon by all the other hunters I knew. The motto
that was constantly preached was "if its brown, its
down"; this bugged me to no end.

Now, I am not saying I haven't shot any young
bucks prior to 1999. I have, but I'd rather shoot a doe

than a small immature buck. But after I made the decision to harvest only mature bucks, I could never quite wrap my head around the small buck-killing attitude.

Thinking back at every single small buck I let pass by, the things I have learned from these young animals have been invaluable. Experiences like that are not ones that can be taught at seminars. It's like everything else in life; experience in a situation always *trumps* philosophy, rumor, hearsay or popular opinion.

If you want to start practicing QDMA, one of the simplest ways is to establish a central mineral site. Some people might think this is unnecessary; but it is the cheapest and easiest way to start the healthy-herd model, and is really the beginning of any successful deer management program.

I attended a QDMA seminar and began to look at different deer-mineral brands. After my research, I decided to purchase Lucky Buck Deer Mineral, the most popular brand in the industry at that time.

I used 5 buckets of Lucky Buck, spaced out every two months from January through October. I did this for five straight years.

Yes, you read that right – five *years*!

Over that time period, I had much better results than not doing anything at all. I was happy with the performance of the product, even though I had no other brand to compare it to.

When I started using Lucky Buck, I noticed there was an increase in activity as well as more deer on camera, though I never got any photos of large bucks.

One day at a local hardware store, I picked up a business card that advertised a new deer-mineral mix from a company in the area. I scanned the card, and decided to dial the phone number out of curiosity.

A man named Jack Hadley Jr. answered right away. I was impressed with the knowledge he had about his all-natural deer-mineral mix. Shortly after our conversation, I purchased my first batch of his mix. I had high hopes that his mix would outperform the current one I was using.

While I was satisfied with my purchase of Lucky Buck, I know the importance of quality products. In my experience, if I want the best results, it's important for me to invest both my time and money.

Even more intrigued, I wanted to see how Massive Mineral Mix would perform against other leading brands, so I decided to conduct my own experiment. I drove to the sporting goods store, purchased three other brands that were bestsellers at the time, and came up with a plan to compare Massive Mineral Mix with others in the industry.

I took those four minerals to 80 acres of woods that I had never hunted before. I did not use cameras because I was nervous about getting them stolen. My experiment was going to be solely based on the deer activity at each mineral site.

I poured the three other leading brands down in areas where there were heavy deer trails and placed each mineral site 10-acres from each other. Then I placed Jack Hadley Jr.'s Massive Mineral Mix on a 10-acre parcel with the least amount of visible deer activity. I experimented with this late in the winter, before springtime was in full force.

Three months later, my friend Jason Merwin and I set out for the woods, eager to see how all the mineral sites turned out. The property was now very green and grown-up. The woods looked completely different because of the springtime foliage.

We quickly came upon the first mineral site. I noted that it had a decent amount of the ground dug out and was trampled with deer tracks. The second mineral site was lightly dug out, indicating very little deer activity.

The third mineral site was a total disappointment. Here, I used a mineral mix that was one of the largest advertised brands. I was totally shocked to see that the mineral had molded! It even had a rotten smell to it. To top it off, it was totally untouched, and this mineral was spread along the heaviest-traveled deer trail. Knowing that it was the most expensive brand that yielded the least amount of return on my investment made me sick to my stomach.

Lastly, I went to check on Jack Hadley Jr.'s Massive Mineral Mix. Jason and I were both in shock and awe. We looked at each other in amazement, not believing what we were seeing!

We quickly ran over to see the carnage. It looked like a war zone. There were trees uprooted, grass demolished, dirt and mud hurled everywhere! The area was so trampled and dug up, it looked like a rodeo had taken place! We were stunned and very excited.

At that moment, I knew the only deer-mineral mix that I would ever invest in would be Jack Hadley Jr.'s Massive Mineral Mix.

CHAPTER 5

All the Other Bucks Suck, New Years' Day 2012

Michigan winters are not easy to weather, and this one was no exception. It was rough, and I hadn't seen my Brow Tine Buck in a couple of years. I honestly thought he was dead.

The upside to scouting deer in the winter months is that you can see exactly where the deer are traveling, with their tracks visible in the snowfall.

I realize mature bucks might not stay true to these trails the entire year. But I can get a general idea, and possibly persuade them to pop up at specific locations.

I decided to create a brand-new Massive Mineral Mix site less than 100 yards from my parents' barn. There is an old apple orchard to the west, and a large swamp to the northwest. And even though the spot I was contemplating was close to homes and near loud and abnormal activity, I decided that establishing a honey hole in this area was worth a shot.

I cleared a 6' x 6' area under a tree with a branch that hangs over the mineral site. I did this since bucks like to chew and get their antlers in with the branches.

It never hurts to try something new, so I poured out a batch of Jack Hadley Jr.'s Massive Mineral Mix, hung up a trail camera, and walked away with an optimistic attitude.

I returned after eight weeks to my newly established mineral site, and discovered that it was torn to pieces. I was shocked and very excited to see what the trail camera would produce!

Quickly, I poured out another batch of Massive Mineral Mix and began to scroll through the photos that filled the camera. I immediately saw two deer that were very large and took charge. Both deer were bucks that had already shed their antlers.

I had never seen the first buck before. But by the way its body was shaped, I was fairly certain he was four or five years old. The second buck slightly stunned me. It was a huge framed deer, but it wasn't very long. It was very wide at the hips and chest. This deer was a beast. It also seemed to pose for the trail camera. He had the same stance every time he would visit and get his fix of Massive Mineral Mix for the day. His actions and body looked very familiar. I studied this buck, and then recognized him!

Even without a head full of bone, the Brow Tine Buck had returned.

I was overcome with emotion at this realization. With all our previous encounters, and my history with this deer, I was really stoked to see that this buck hit my new Massive Mineral Mix site every three to four days for the entire eight weeks.

All my concern and worry over this buck instantly disappeared. A new chapter was beginning, and with many more tools in my toolbox. I was on a search mission for this deer, and I wanted to harvest a great one. Now, with the coming bow season, the chase was on!

I felt so grateful for the new friendship I had with Jack Hadley Jr., and I was very impressed with his healthy mineral product.

Jack is one of a kind. He is a hardworking entrepreneur and sportsman, but also down-to-earth and easy to talk to. He knows how to create awesome products, and he is an exceptional hunter as well. He is eager to share his experience and hunting stories. He showed me all the different animals he harvested over the years, and told me stories of the people he has learned from.

Because of his experience, knowledge, and results, the decision was easy to make him my go-to guy for hunting advice. Since then, my opinion of Jack has not wavered. He always strives to give his customers the best, and he doesn't hold anything back. He really is in a class of his own.

CHAPTER 6

The Zombie Deer,
September 2012

Entering the summer of 2012, things started to feel more real than ever before.

The excitement and anticipation for the upcoming bow season was heavy. It began to feel like it couldn't come fast enough. My tree stand was ready, and I was eager to hunt my buck.

At this point, I was shooting my bow regularly with confidence. Through the trail camera, I was seeing my buck grow an impressive eight-point rack. The mass of his rack was quite remarkable, and his body was tipping Goliath in size. He was no longer the scared, wide-eyed buck I once knew. He was mature, and ready to harvest.

Continuing to scout him, I memorized his pattern and activity. He often ran alongside another buck that was a beautiful nine-point. But I had absolutely no care in the world for his running mate. He would make another hunter very happy and he was equally as beautiful as my Brow Tine Buck, but I didn't have a history with him, so I just wasn't interested in him. I was in pursuit of my Brow Tine Buck, and it was time to get it done.

August rolled around, and something strange happened. I began to notice the drop-off in deer camera photos throughout the entire woods. I wasn't alone in my observations; friends and fellow hunters were in agreement with me. It was like a spaceship flew overhead, abducted all the deer, and flew away. I was nervous that my Brow Tine Buck was included in this mysterious deer raid, and we all wanted answers.

It wasn't long before the woods became a ghost town. Coyotes, squirrels, and raccoons were the only feature presentations on my computer. The drop-off in deer activity was nearly unbelievable, and we were all hoping it was a hoax.

As all this was happening, my dad and I, along with two of my cousins, Jonathon and Christopher Coblentz, went fishing for smallmouth bass on the Kalamazoo River. We had a great time catching fish for the first few hours, then came around a river bend and decided to take a break for lunch.

As my dad and I were in the canoe a few minutes ahead, we waited for my cousins to catch up with us and anchor down. We waited and waited, but there was no sign of them anywhere.

I decided to call them to see what was going on. As I chatted with Chris, I heard a bit of adrenaline in his voice as he told me about this huge buck that walked down from the riverbank right before their eyes, fell into the water, and drowned itself in the river while its rack slowly disappeared.

I was totally confused by what he was trying to tell me. He described a giant wall-hanger buck staggering like a drunkard, falling into the river, disappearing, and sadly drowning. I have never heard of anything like this in my life. We were aware that there was some sort of disease in the area that was killing off our deer, but as far as I knew, we had not received any word or detailed information from authorities.

The following day, Jonathon was back at the Kalamazoo River, fishing with a friend of his. He retold he story of the giant zombie-like eight-point. As he was describing the events that occurred, he noticed a large buck stuck on a rock near the riverbend water rapids. Narrowing his gaze, he was surprised to see that it was the same zombie-like buck from the previous day!

He quickly called Chris, who happened to be working with me that day. Jonathon described the scene to us, and asked that we come with equipment to get the rack. We also called the Department of Natural Resources (DNR) right after we hung up.

We immediately dropped our tools and rushed toward the river grabbing a hacksaw, rubber gloves, garbage bags and a canoe. We paddled that canoe faster than a cheetah running after his prey in order to see this unique incident.

As we reached the river, we immediately noticed (and smelled) the dead buck. The smell was unbelievably wretched and abhorrent, and made us nauseous. We anchored down and wished we grabbed our gas masks to cover our faces.

We began to realize even more how horrible this disease was becoming. It was disgusting and very sad to see this buck with hardly any skin on his face. He looked like something from *The Walking Dead*.

Feeling unsettled, I wondered how many more zombie deer were staggering to the nearest watering hole.

We talked to some local hunters in the days that followed. Stories of dead deer were swarming our area like an apocalypse was happening. This is when things started to make more sense.

One young man in particular told me that he, along with the Michigan DNR, dragged over 100 white-tailed deer from his 150-acre property, and he had pictures and video to prove it. During that time, the Michigan DNR stated that *Epizootic Hemorrhagic Disease or EHD in white-tailed deer* had hit our area really hard, especially along rivers, creeks, ponds, and lakes.

According to the State of Michigan website (https://www.michigan.gov/ehd), EHD is an acute, infectious, and often fatal viral disease of some wild ruminants. This malady, characterized by extensive hemorrhages, has been responsible for significant epizootics in deer in the northern United States and southern Canada. A similar hemorrhagic disease called bluetongue also occurs throughout North America. The two diseases are antigenically different.

My heart sank at this knowledge. Reality set in, and I now understood why there was not a single deer in sight, and no evidence of the Brow Tine Buck and his nine-point running mate. I realized that the buck I had invested so much time in was a thing of the past.

Because my only two hunting properties were along rivers, creeks, and swamps, things felt utterly hopeless, not just for this bow season, but (I figured) for many years to come. I prayed that the Lord would have at least spared my buck, the one and only deer I have had my sights on for all these years.

CHAPTER 7

Bow Season is Now Open, October 1, 2012

I was not optimistic on the opening morning of the 2012 bow season. My mind was filled with all that I had found about EHD. I had little to no confidence in seeing deer, let alone killing one.

Sitting in my stand, I had the perfect spot. I watched the sun rise, and felt the northwest wind begin to blow across a wet 100-acre swamp. It would have been a perfect opening morning had it not been for the smell of dead deer carcass swirling throughout the woods.

By 8:30 am, the foul smells became so wretched. It was, hands down, the most horrible smell I have ever experienced.

I got my phone out and called my dad. I told him what was going on, and fumed about the stupid disease that plagued our woods. The aroma was so grotesque that I imagined countless dead deer lying in the middle of the swamp, decaying.

Irritated, I packed up my gear and headed home to deliberate. Consulting with myself, I was committed to stick to my original plan. *I'm a hunter*, I thought. *A sportsman. I will not be defeated. I'm going to continue down my path like I normally do, take note of what I discover in the woods, and adjust accordingly.*

I continued to hunt week after week, with no sign of deer. I had not taken a single photo, nor found any deer tracks. Keep in mind that I am only talking about two different 30-acre parcels that are only five miles apart. Both properties border swamps and mainstream rivers.

This limited hunting space was a major source of my frustration. It's not like I was overhunting a single area. I would move from stand to stand, even hunting the ground. I made sure there was lots of cover, and I used the wind as my guide. All things considered, it just seemed hopeless.

With the last day of early bow season coming to an end, and the opening day of shotgun season starting the next morning, I was severely discouraged. Imagining my trek out on one of the most anticipated days of the year, thinking it is going to just be a waste of time, was depressing.

All of the positive thinking and motivational tactics I learned over the years was no match for this experience. The bottom line is that hunting for weeks, with nothing to show for it, beats you up mentally.

Hunting isn't easy, especially when you see absolutely zero deer. Bow season might have been an official bust, but I've never been a quitter, and didn't plan to start quitting now. I decided to march into shotgun season with all the fierceness it deserved.

CHAPTER 8

Opening Morning of the 2012 Firearm Season

Sitting in my tree stand on the morning of the 2012 opening day of firearm season, the swamp of death taunted me. As I sat there, I began to mull over the previous night, when a group of us got together for dinner. I pondered their hunting stories and remembered how they enthusiastically talked about the mature bucks they were scouting, and how there was a feeding frenzy on their property over Jack's Massive Mineral Mix.

I enjoyed listening to their stories and was eager to engage in the conversation in spite of the sting in my gut. I reminded myself that evening that I had done everything I could to maintain a healthy deer herd with the resources I had.

My Brow Tine Buck and his comrade had been smashing Jack's Massive Mineral Mix religiously for an entire year. I was holding on to a tiny glimmer of hope that perhaps he survived the EHD outbreak and was healthy.

Stuffing my knowledge of EHD to the back of my mind, I pressed on and envisioned my Brow Tine Buck reappearing once again.

I silently listened to the season's first gunshots firing in the distance. I felt exhilarated. My neighboring hunters were not shooting at squirrels; those were deer shots. My optimism returned as I heard those shots come closer and closer over the next hour.

I hear a dozen different shots circling many acres around me. Then it was silent for about 30 minutes. I texted my dad and other local hunters to find out who was shooting, and what everyone was seeing. I continued to hear activity throughout the woods while patiently waiting. Voices and ATVs echoed through the trees.

Suddenly, I heard something from the east crashing through the swamp, heavy-footed like a rhino. It drew closer and closer, but I couldn't see anything yet. Nearer and nearer it crept, until it finally emerged.

There he was, a beautiful heavy-racked buck. I watched him for a moment, only to watch him disappear quickly into the thickest area of the swamp.

With my adrenaline racing, I gave a couple of low grunts. Almost immediately, the buck ran back out right in front of me, looking for a fight. Breathing heavily, I readied my shotgun. My 12-gauge, single-shot Harrington and Richardson weapon with a Barska scope sat securely on my gun rest as I keyed in on the beast.

Inching forward, he landed full focus on my crosshairs and, with the sound of my own voice saying "Errrr", I made him stop in his tracks.

The thick-bodied buck turned his head toward me and posed in a stance that I had seen before. My heart began to pound as I recalled my many months worth of thoughts, feelings, prayers, scouting and determination. What I hoped for was now my reality.

I scanned his body and stature in disbelief. I *knew* that I knew him. As my brain fought to make sense of this familiar buck, I realized it was *the* Brow Tine Buck. *My* Brow Tine Buck, the same one I had been scouting for nearly five years.

There he was, a 6½-year-old mature buck, surprising me again by his very presence.

I placed my finger on the trigger while recollecting all of my moments with him over the years. I whispered to myself, *This is now my buck.*

Excitement laced with force and confidence as I pulled the trigger. The Hornady 300 grain sabot slug hit its mark; and I watched the legendary, over-220-pound buck drop to the ground without a twitch.

I stared at him with disbelief from 80 yards away. I felt as if I had accomplished the impossible.

I did it! I thought. *I shot the deer that I had been praying for for years!*

I sat there stunned. My mind felt frozen. I looked blankly at my kill. Epiphany set in. Determination. Commitment. Perseverance. I believe the Lord had a plan this entire time, and the last part of my journey couldn't have been any sweeter. This reward was truly worth the wait.

My dad was calling, and I was returned to reality by my vibrating phone. Enthusiastically, I shared my exciting news with him and asked that he come right away. I calmed my excitement and climbed down from the tree stand.

It felt like an eternity before I could reach the Brow Tine Buck. Approaching him, I was dumbfounded and quiet, soaking it all in the best I could.

My dad joined me, and together we stood there staring at him. We were speechless, yet excited to see that the Brow Tine Buck made it through the EHD outbreak healthy and alive.

At that moment, two thoughts filled my head.

The first one was the advice my uncle Reuben Coblentz gave me. He is from Ohio and he has harvested a few monster deer with a Boone & Crockett score of over 180 inches. He is an impressive hunter. I had asked him what he feels like after he shoots these massive, world-class bucks. He told me this: "Take your time, grab ahold of his rack, and don't just rush out of the woods. Enjoy every part of that hunt and kill. You might never have a buck that big or that meaningful again in your lifetime, so soak it all in."

While my buck may not have scored nearly as high as most of his, it was the most meaningful deer I had ever shot. In that moment, I took his advice to heart.

As I grabbed hold of my buck's rack, my second thought had to do with the health and wellness of this beast. I was convinced that Jack's Massive Mineral Mix had not only helped this buck survive, but also thrive. Evidence of this was his thick body and his undeniably larger rack. It was impressive.

After more research, my anecdotal evidence showed that this buck made it through the disease totally fine and healthy. There is no other reason for me to have any other evaluation. A healthy herd and a more massive rack are what were advertised and proven, and I'm buying every bit.

The State of Michigan website has the following statement regarding the treatment and control of EHD:

> There is no known effective treatment or control of EHD. Theoretically, an **oral** vaccine could be developed for administration through a **supplementary winter feeding**

program, but this is presently impossible, impractical, and unwarranted.

Maybe the Michigan state government should read my story.

We dragged my buck to an abandoned old railroad bed. It was a struggle due to his massive size.

As my dad walked back to the house to bring the Bobcat skid-steer loader to make it easier to haul him back home, he found out from a neighbor that my Brow Tine Buck's big nine-point running mate was shot and killed. The only two deer devouring Massive Mineral Mix survived the EHD outbreak, go figure!

As I stayed back in the woods alone for a while, I prayed. I thanked Jesus for not only guiding my Hornady bullet for an absolutely perfect shot, but also the opportunity to hunt with my dad, and have such an awesome experience.

We take so many things, moments, chances and people we may meet for granted. Had I not found Jack's business card and actually called him, I would not have had this amazing and memorable experience. I owe so much of this hunting success story to him and his company, Massive Mineral Mix. I'm forever grateful to and for him.

CONCLUSION

All we can do as outdoorsmen is the best we can, with the resources we have, at any given time. To me, this hunting experience is a reminder of hope and perseverance, and the amazing things that can happen when I stick to my God-given beliefs and talents.

This story is about hope in things that cannot be seen. I could have quit at any time, but I didn't. And because I didn't quit, I am now able to share this amazing story with you. My hope is that this story brings you encouragement.

I believe nothing is accidental, incidental, or coincidental. I believe my purpose in life is to honor the Lord with my talents, and in every situation.

Whatever answers your looking for, you can find those answers in Jesus Christ.

Brokenness, betrayal, shame, guilt, addiction, and every single sin can be given to the Heavenly Father because He does not want you to be chained down by them. He wants you to have healing, restoration, and freedom.

I owe everything I have ever done in my Life to Jesus. He has given me new life, and life more abundantly. This hunting experience reminds me of a couple of my favorite Bible verses.

Romans 8:25:

But if we hope for that we see not, then do we with patience wait for it.

Matthew 17:20:

And Jesus said unto them, Because of your **unbelief**: for verily I say unto you, if ye have **faith as a grain of mustard seed,** ye shall say unto this mountain, Remove hence to yonder place; and it shall remove; and **nothing shall be impossible unto you**.

What these mean are that it only takes a little bit of faith in Jesus and to stand firm on the Word of God (the Bible). These principles of God's word give us the faith of his promises. God cannot fail and does not give us a spirit of fear, but of a sound mind. I encourage you to accept Jesus as your personal savior. He has changed my entire life and how I look though a different lens. There is no shame in Jesus Christ.

Maybe you have done things or made decisions that you regret. We all have. If you feel a heavy weight for those decisions, you should know that life can start brand new for you right now, at this very moment.

A question for you to ask yourself is this, "Is my heart right with God"?

If you say "I don't know" or "I think so, but I'm not sure", then today you can know for sure. Knowing for sure gives you freedom and the Lord's promises.

We have to admit that we are all sinners and we need what Jesus did on the cross for us to be saved from eternity in Hell. He took on all the sins of the world, for you and me.

Ephesians 2:8-9: For by grace are ye saved through faith; and that not of yourselves: it is the gift of God: Not of works, lest any man should boast.

Romans 3:23 says that "For *all* have sinned, and come short of the glory of God".

This means that being a good person and simply doing good works will not give you eternity in Heaven. We ALL sin, and are not able to live a perfect life.

Romans 10:9 says "That if thou shalt confess with thy mouth the Lord Jesus, and shalt believe in thine heart that God hath raised him from the dead, thou shalt be saved".

This means there has to be a moment where you call upon the name of the Lord, and you will be saved.

If you would like to accept Jesus as your personal savior, then you can express this directly to him in prayer. You can use my words below, or use your own.

Oh Heavenly Father,

Forgive me for all my sins. Make me brand-new. Jesus, be my savior and the Lord of my life. Fill me with your spirit so I can serve you, so I can follow you, so I can make you known. My life is not my own; I give it to you.

Thank you for new life. I give you mine.

In Jesus' name, I pray,

Amen.

If you put your trust in Jesus, prayed and meant it, then this is the greatest prayer you will ever pray.

Please feel free to share your story with me, and I would be happy to help you get connected with a church in your area. I love hearing about new life transformations. I will try and help you the best I can.

When you are united with Jesus in faith, you can begin to move mountains.

Resources

If you have any questions about this story or if you're interested in any of Joseph Byler's coaching services, find him at www.crosscutyourlife.com or call 517-937-6557. He loves meeting new people, and is ready to help or guide individuals any way he can. He is on Instagram and Twitter as @bylerzone.

For more information on Jack Hadley Jr.'s Massive Mineral Mix, or how to be a distributor of Massive Mineral Mix, go to www.massivemineral.com or call Jack himself at 517-525-1407. Jack will answer any questions you may have about his product.

He also owns Armor Insulation (www.insulatewitharmor.com), which caters to your insulation needs. He is honest, and always over-delivers. He is on Facebook and Instagram as @massivemineralmix, and on Twitter as @massivemineral.

If you're interested in learning more about QDMA, check out your state's regulations on deer mineral and how to start your own QDMA program with the very best and proven deer-mineral product on the market.

Thank you for reading this story. Get inspired, keep the faith, and may the Lord bless you.

Made in the USA
Monee, IL
11 December 2019